In the Spotlight

Oprah Winfrey

by Kaitlyn Duling

Bullfrog
Books

Ideas for Parents and Teachers

Bullfrog Books let children practice reading informational text at the earliest reading levels. Repetition, familiar words, and photo labels support early readers.

Before Reading

- Discuss the cover photo. What does it tell them?

- Look at the picture glossary together. Read and discuss the words.

Read the Book

- "Walk" through the book and look at the photos. Let the child ask questions. Point out the photo labels.

- Read the book to the child, or have him or her read independently.

After Reading

- Prompt the child to think more. Ask: What did you know about Oprah Winfrey before reading this book? What more would you like to learn about her after reading it?

Bullfrog Books are published by Jump!
5357 Penn Avenue South
Minneapolis, MN 55419
www.jumplibrary.com

Library of Congress Cataloging-in-Publication Data is available at www.loc.gov or upon request from the publisher.

ISBN: 978-1-64128-213-0 (hardcover)
ISBN: 978-1-64128-214-7 (paperback)
ISBN: 978-1-64128-215-4 (ebook)

Editors: Susanne Bushman & Kristine Spanier
Designer: Molly Ballanger

Photo Credits: Jeff Vespa/Getty, cover; Kathy Hutchins/Shutterstock, 1; Peter Kramer/Getty, 3; Michael Tran/Getty, 4; Brooks Kraft/Getty, 5, 23br; Brendon Thorne/Getty, 6–7, 2tm; Collection Christophel/Alamy, 8; Alberto E. Rodriguez/Getty, 9; Benny Gool/AP Images, 10–11; Kevin Mazur/Getty, 12–13, 23tl; AFP/Getty, 14; Per-Anders Pettersson/Getty, 15; Rob Crandall/Shutterstock, 16, 22tr, 23bl; David Hume Kennerly/Getty, 16–17; Scott Olson/Getty, 18–19, 23tr; Megan Ngan/Getty, 20–21; kak2s/Shutterstock, 22tl; Twin Design/Shutterstock, 22bl; Collection Christophel/Alamy, 22br; Wead/Shutterstock, 23bm; SGranitz/Getty, 24.

Printed in the United States of America at Corporate Graphics in North Mankato, Minnesota.

Table of Contents

Oprah

This is Oprah!

She has had many jobs.
She started on TV.

Jay-Z

She had a talk show.

It was on for
25 years.

She had many
famous guests.

Wow!

Oprah acts.

She is in movies.

She has a magazine.

She writes books.

She wants people
to read more.

People love Oprah.
She is kind.
She is generous.

Oprah donates money.

She raises it, too.

For what?

People who need homes.
Or medicine.

DONATE NOW

13

Oprah opened a school.
It is in South Africa.

She helps
girls learn.

15

She gives to museums.
Nice!

museum

NATIONAL MUSEUM *of* AFRICAN AMERICAN HISTORY & CULTURE

Smithsonian

17

She works hard.

She listens.

She speaks out.

19

Oprah inspires us.

The president gave her an award for it.

She wants people to live their best lives.

President
Obama

Medal of
Freedom

21

Key Events

January 29, 1954:
Oprah Gail Winfrey is born in Kosciusko, Mississippi.

September 8, 1986:
The Oprah Winfrey Show airs on national television.

June 11, 2013:
Oprah announces a $12 million donation to the Smithsonian National Museum of African American History and Culture.

January 2, 1984:
Oprah hosts her first episode of the talk show *AM Chicago.*

January 2, 2007:
The Oprah Winfrey Leadership Academy for Girls opens in South Africa.

February 26, 2018:
A Wrinkle in Time, starring Oprah as Mrs. Which, is released in the United States.

Picture Glossary

donates
Gives something, such as money, to a charity.

famous
Very well-known to many people.

inspires
Influences and encourages people to achieve or do something.

museums
Places where objects are preserved and displayed.

South Africa
A country on the southern tip of the continent of Africa.

talk show
A program on which people discuss important topics.

Index

To Learn More

Finding more information is as easy as 1, 2, 3.

❶ Go to www.factsurfer.com

❷ Enter "OprahWinfrey" into the search box.

❸ Click the "Surf" button to see a list of websites.